THE TABERNACLE

Rose Visual
Bible Studies

HENDRICKSON PUBLISHERS   ROSE PUBLISHING

The Tabernacle
Rose Visual Bible Studies

©2018 Rose Publishing, LLC

Rose Publishing, LLC
P.O. Box 3473
Peabody, Massachusetts 01961-3473 USA
www.hendricksonrose.com

All rights reserved. No part of this work may be reproduced or transmitted in any form or by any means, electronic or mechanical, including photocopying, recording, or by any information storage and retrieval system, without permission in writing from the publisher.

Scriptures taken from the Holy Bible, New International Version®, NIV®. Copyright © 1973, 1978, 1984, 2011 by Biblica, Inc.™ Used by permission of Zondervan. All rights reserved worldwide. www.zondervan.com. The "NIV" and "New International Version" are trademarks registered in the United States Patent and Trademark Office by Biblica, Inc.™

Scripture quotations marked NLT are taken from the Holy Bible, New Living Translation, copyright ©1996, 2004, 2007, 2013, 2015 by Tyndale House Foundation. Used by permission of Tyndale House Publishers, Inc., Carol Stream, Illinois 60188. All rights reserved.

Scripture quotations marked ESV are from the ESV® Bible (The Holy Bible, English Standard Version®), copyright © 2001 by Crossway, a publishing ministry of Good News Publishers. Used by permission. All rights reserved.

Adapted from *Rose Guide to the Tabernacle* by Rose Publishing.

Book design by Cristalle Kishi.

Photographs used under license from Shutterstock.com, Lightstock, LLC, and Dreamstime. Tabernacle illustrations by Jerry Allison, Stan Stein, and Cara Nilsen.

Printed in the United States of America
010418VP

Contents

1 GOD WITH US
A Sanctuary in the Wilderness
Page 7

2 SACRIFICE & HOLINESS
The Altar of Burnt Offering
The Laver
Page 23

3 LIGHT IN A DARK PLACE
The Lampstand
Page 39

4 GOD'S INVITATION
The Table of Bread
The Altar of Incense
Page 53

5 DRAWING NEAR TO GOD
The Veil
The Ark of the Covenant
Page 67

6 FINDING MERCY
The High Priest
The Mercy Seat
Page 83

LEADER'S GUIDE
Page 97

*"Have them make
a sanctuary for me,
and I will dwell among them."*

Exodus 25:8

The Tabernacle

How can a holy God dwell among a sinful people? That's the question the Israelites asked in the wilderness centuries ago. And it's a question we still ask today.

Sin separates us from God. It damages relationships. It makes us impure, and it corrupts the life that God intends for his creation. As the Old Testament prophet Isaiah says, "It's your sins that have cut you off from God" (59:2 NLT).

Yet we know from the Bible that God *did* live among his people—and that he is *near* to us today. How can this be?

In this study of the tabernacle, you'll see how everything about the tabernacle—from the outer courtyard to the innermost sacred place—points to this truth: Our holy Creator has chosen to dwell with his fallen creation and restore us from the brokenness that sin has caused. He has made a way for this to be possible.

Yet the tabernacle is many centuries gone. The book of Hebrews explains that the ancient things we read about in the Old Testament are "only a shadow of the good things that are coming—not the realities themselves" (10:1). The tabernacle pointed people toward something else—or *someone* else. As a shadow indicates the existence of a real object, so the tabernacle indicates that there is a real, eternal pathway to God. But unlike the ancient tabernacle activities, this way is not a set of religious practices and rituals; those can never truly save us from sin. This way is a person. It's the person who came to earth 2,000 years ago and declared, "I am the way, the truth, and the life" (John 14:6).

1
GOD WITH US

A Sanctuary in the Wilderness

God with Us

They were God's people—journeying through the wilderness, far from the only home they had known in Egypt. They had left their lives of slavery in Egypt to follow God's promise to give them a new land, a promised land they could call home. God had shown them that he was with them and on their side when he delivered them out of Pharaoh's grip. But would God still be with them as they traveled for years through the desert?

On this journey, the people doubted, they grumbled, and at times they sinned gravely. Yet God provided for their needs, both physical and spiritual. He was always with them.

As a visible, tangible reminder that he dwelt among his people wherever they went, God commanded them to build a sanctuary called a tabernacle. But this was no ordinary worship center; it was God's holy sanctuary. Situated in the middle of their camp, the tabernacle would be a constant reminder to everyone that God dwelt among them. The people of earth could commune with the God of heaven!

Read It

Key Bible Passages

Exodus 25:1–9

John 1:1–14

Optional Reading

Exodus 26:1–37

Hebrews 8:1–13

The *Key Bible Passage* is the main reading for each session. The *Optional Reading* will take you further, through Old Testament passages about the tabernacle as well as New Testament passages about how Jesus fulfilled what the tabernacle foreshadowed.

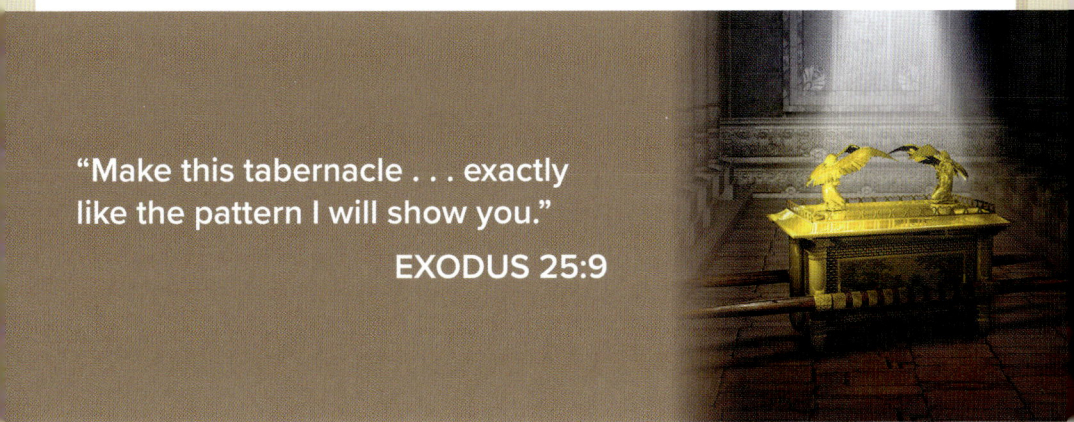

> "Make this tabernacle . . . exactly like the pattern I will show you."
>
> **EXODUS 25:9**

Know It

1. From your reading in the book of Exodus, what stood out to you as significant about the tabernacle?

2. What does it mean that Jesus (the Word) "made his dwelling among us" (John 1:14)?

3. Imagine you were one of the ancient Israelites in the wilderness. How might you have responded when Moses said that God told him to build a special tent—a sanctuary for God—in the desert?

   ❏ Eager to get started

   ❏ Skeptical

   ❏ Want no part of building it

   ❏ Ready to donate personal belongings to it

   ❏ Willing but reluctant to participate

   ❏ Feel grateful to God

   ❏ Think Moses is crazy!

   ❏ Other: _____

Explore It

Timeline

1876 BC
For about 400 years, the people of Israel (called Hebrews in the book of Exodus) live in Egypt. For part of that time, they are forced into slavery by the pharaoh.

1526 BC
Moses is born in Egypt to a Hebrew slave. He is placed in a basket in the Nile to avoid Pharaoh's decree that all Hebrew male babies be killed. Moses is found by Pharaoh's daughter, who raises him as a prince of Egypt.

C. 1486 BC
Moses flees Egypt after killing an Egyptian man who was beating a Hebrew slave.

1446 BC
God speaks to Moses from a burning bush and sends Moses back to Egypt to liberate the Hebrew slaves.

After God sends ten devastating plagues upon Egypt, Pharaoh relents, and the Hebrews leave Egypt, escaping through the Red Sea which God miraculously parts for them.

God leads the people into Sinai, where he gives Moses the tablets of the law and instructions for building the tabernacle.

The people build the tabernacle as God instructed. Moses' brother Aaron becomes the first high priest serving in the tabernacle.

(Continued on next page.)

1446–1406 BC
God's people spend 40 years in the wilderness as he leads them with a cloud by day and a pillar of fire by night. The people take the portable tabernacle with them wherever they journey.

1406 BC
Moses dies on Mt. Nebo at the edge of the promised land.

Joshua succeeds Moses and leads the Israelites into the promised land.

(Dates are approximate.)

No one knows for sure where Mt. Sinai described in Exodus is located, but the traditional site is at the southernmost end of the Sinai Peninsula where St. Catherine's Monastery (shown here) was built in the sixth century AD.

The Tent of Meeting

Before the tabernacle was completed, Moses had built a similar—but much simpler—structure. It was called the "tent of meeting" (Exodus 33:7) because it was the place where Moses met with God to receive divine guidance as he led the people. This tent was a makeshift structure that was incorporated into the tabernacle when it was constructed. Many years later, the tabernacle itself would be incorporated into the temple built by King Solomon in Jerusalem.

Three Parts of the Tabernacle

The tabernacle had three main sections, each containing special, sacred objects. Each section was also the place of different sacred activities.

1. THE COURTYARD

This was the place where people would bring their sacrifices and offerings. They would enter through the wide gate on the east and would be welcomed by the priests, who would carry out the sacrifices at the altar of burnt offering. There was also a laver, in which the priests could wash themselves to be ritually clean.

2. THE HOLY PLACE

This first room housed three important objects:

- The lampstand
- The table of the bread of presence (table of showbread)
- The altar of incense

The priests performed daily tasks inside the Holy Place. They kept the lamps burning, offered incense twice a day, and brought fresh bread weekly to the table.

3. THE MOST HOLY PLACE

Also called the Holy of Holies, this second room in the tent was a unique inner sanctuary. The ark of the covenant was in this room. God's very presence dwelt in the Most Holy Place. Only the high priest could enter this room once a year, protected by a cloud of smoke from burnt incense. This room was central to the most important celebration in the Jewish calendar, the Day of Atonement. On this day, the high priest offered the blood of a sacrificed animal on the ark of the covenant to atone for the people's sin.

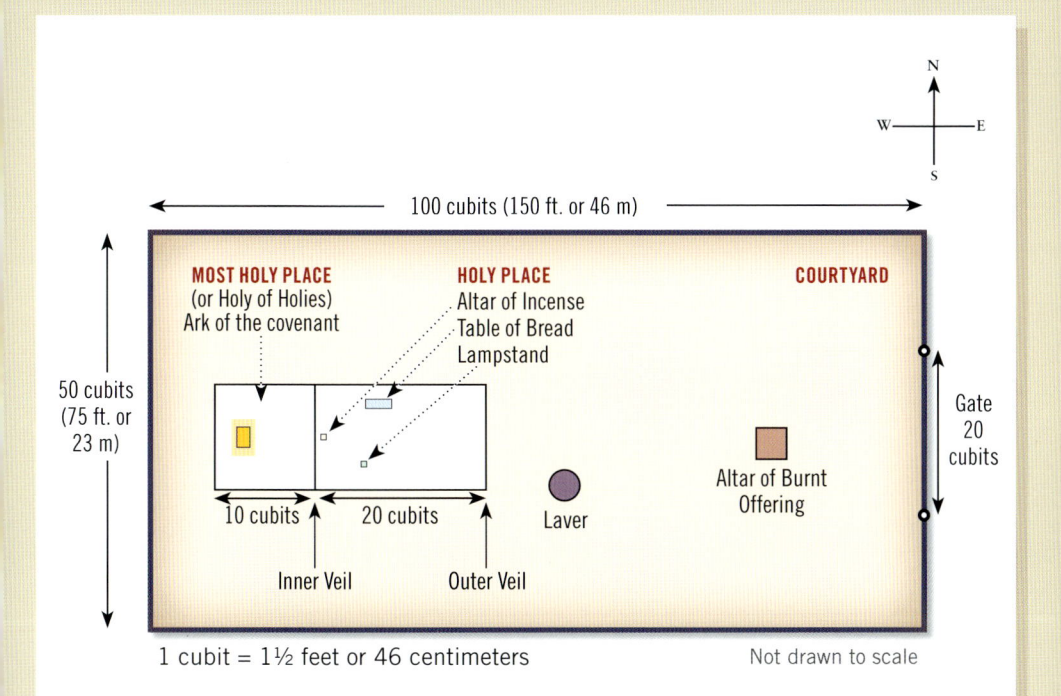

100 cubits (150 ft. or 46 m)

50 cubits (75 ft. or 23 m)

MOST HOLY PLACE (or Holy of Holies)
Ark of the covenant

HOLY PLACE
Altar of Incense
Table of Bread
Lampstand

COURTYARD

10 cubits | 20 cubits

Inner Veil | Outer Veil

Laver

Altar of Burnt Offering

Gate 20 cubits

1 cubit = 1½ feet or 46 centimeters

Not drawn to scale

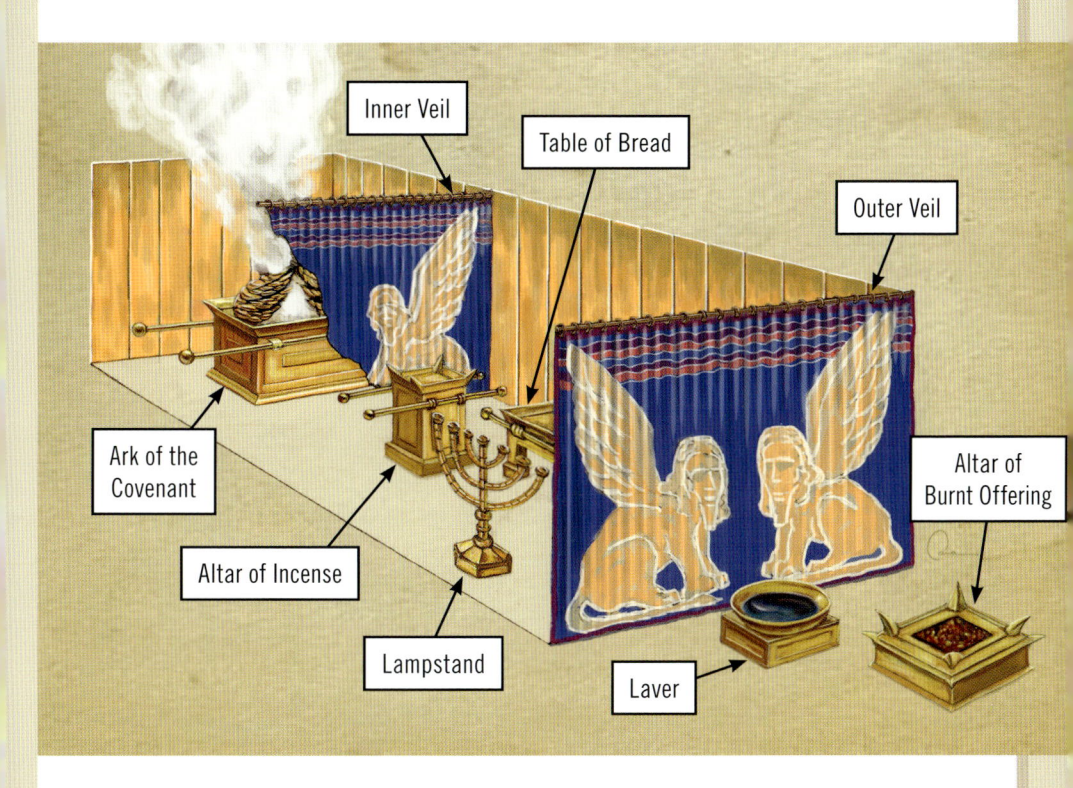

- Inner Veil
- Table of Bread
- Outer Veil
- Ark of the Covenant
- Altar of Incense
- Lampstand
- Laver
- Altar of Burnt Offering

15

Live It

With Us Always

Jesus pitched his tent among us. Does that sound like an unusual thing to say? Well, that's exactly what the apostle John tells readers: "The Word [Jesus] became flesh and made his dwelling among us" (John 1:14). The phrase "made his dwelling" is from the Greek word *eskenosen,* which literally means "pitch a tent."

God had dwelt with his people through a tabernacle, a tent in the wilderness (Exodus 25:8). In coming to earth as a human, Jesus the Son of God lived with us as one of us.

Yet Jesus no longer (literally) walks the earth with his followers as he did 2,000 years ago in Israel. So how is he still dwelling with his followers today? When the resurrected Jesus departed from his disciples on a mountaintop in Galilee, he addressed this very concern. He assured them, "I am with you always, to the very end of the age" (Matthew 28:20).

The apostle Paul knew this to be true. He prayed that God "may strengthen you with power through his Spirit in your inner being, so that Christ may *dwell in your hearts* through faith" (Ephesians 3:16–17, emphasis added). This was true for believers then, and it is still true for believers today. The Son of God has not left us alone; he is *with us* now and forever.

Life Application Questions

1. As you begin this six-session study on the tabernacle, do you see any similarities between the tabernacle and your place of worship? How do the two compare?

2. Read Hebrews 8:5–6. What does it mean that the tabernacle was a *shadow* of something else?

3. Hebrews 10:1 says that the ancient Israelites awaited "good things that are coming." What are some of God's promises that Christians today wait for God to fulfill?

4. When have you sensed God's presence *most* or *least* in your life? What were those experiences like?

5. What challenges do you face in knowing (and feeling) that God is with you every step of the way? What can you do to overcome those challenges?

6. The tabernacle was an expression of God's presence, guidance, and protection. What are some practical ways you can help others understand that God's presence can make a positive difference in their lives?

Prayer

Our heavenly Father,

Your love for humanity is amazing! You have chosen to dwell with your creation. Your Son, Jesus, has promised to be with us *always*.

Help us to know in our heads and feel in our hearts that you are with us every step of the way. You have not left us alone. You have made your dwelling in our lives.

In Jesus' name, amen.

Notes

Notes

2
SACRIFICE & HOLINESS

*The Altar of
Burnt Offering*

The Laver

Sacrifice & Holiness

As we saw in the first session, it was no coincidence that the tabernacle was situated at the center of the Israelite camp. It was God's way of visibly reminding his people that he was with them, right there in their midst.

The items in the tabernacle courtyard and their specific placement were no coincidence either. God was communicating eternal truths through these earthly, temporary objects.

When a person entered the courtyard through its one entrance, the first thing encountered was the altar of burnt offering with its fire and smoke from the daily offerings. The smells of roasted animal flesh or grain and the smoke ascending to heaven, along with the very earthy animal smells, marked this area as a place where earth and heaven touched. It was the place where reconciliation between God and humanity began.

Beyond the altar was the laver filled with fresh water in which the priests washed themselves after offering sacrifices. The laver marked the place of purification for the priests to make them holy. God is a holy God—and his people must be made holy too.

Read It

Key Bible Passages

Exodus 27:1–8; 30:17–21

Titus 2:11–14

1 John 1:7–9

Optional Reading

Exodus 38:1–8

Hebrews 10:1–18

This extra reading from Exodus tells more about where sacrifices were made and where priests purified themselves. The reading from Hebrews tells how Jesus was the last sacrifice.

> "The blood of Jesus, his Son, purifies us from all sin."
>
> **1 JOHN 1:7**

Know It

1. In Exodus 30:20, the priests are instructed to wash with water before entering the Holy Place "so that they will not die." Why do you think they might die if they entered the Holy Place without ceremonially purifying themselves?

2. Imagine yourself as one of the Hebrews in the camp in the wilderness. What might watching the daily sacrifices and the priests' rituals communicate to you about God—and about yourself?

3. Look again at Titus 2:11–14 and 1 John 1:7–9. What is the connection between Jesus' sacrifice and our purity?

Explore It

The Altar of Burnt Offering

- The altar of burnt offering was a hollow frame made of acacia wood and overlaid with bronze. It contained a bronze grate midway up the entire assembly.

- Due to the need for portability, the altar was made with a ring at each corner, and poles could be inserted through the rings, allowing the altar to be carried by the priests.

- The four "horns" on the upper corners symbolized God's power over life and death, and they were points where the blood of the sacrifices was sprinkled.

- The altar was placed by the entrance so that the altar was the first thing seen upon entering the courtyard.

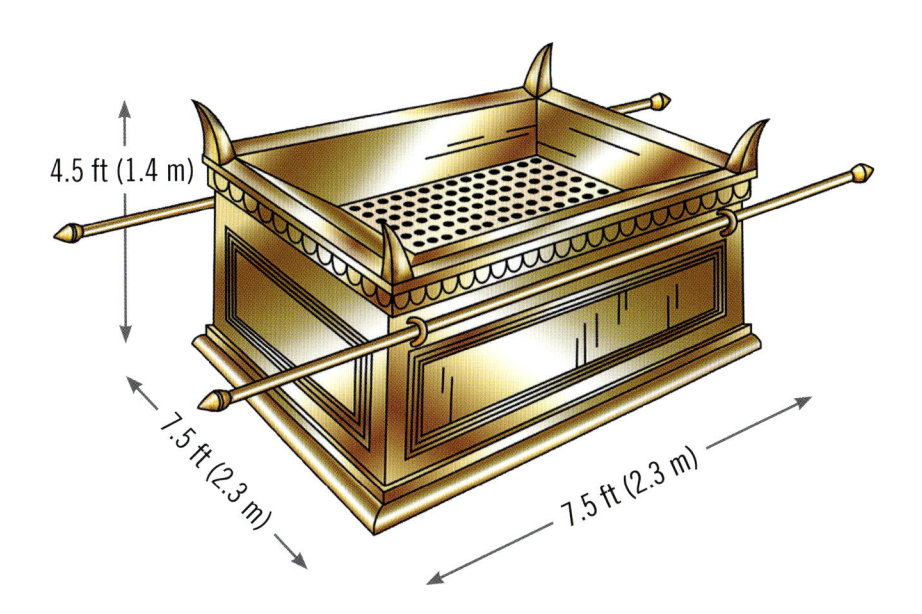

4.5 ft (1.4 m)

7.5 ft (2.3 m)

7.5 ft (2.3 m)

Why Sacrifice?

One of the biggest problems that people today have with the idea of sacrifice is its inevitable bloodiness. Sacrifice today simply appears primitive and cruel. So a brief word about how Old Testament people understood the concept of blood will be helpful.

The first encounter with blood in the Bible occurred when Cain murdered his brother Abel. God voiced the seriousness of Cain's offense: "What have you done? Listen! Your brother's blood cries out to me from the ground" (Genesis 4:10).

In Genesis 9:3–6, God prohibited eating or drinking the blood of animals. The explanation for this prohibition is in Leviticus 17:11: "For the life of a creature is in the blood, and I have given it to you to make atonement for yourselves on the altar; it is the blood that makes atonement for one's life." The blood of animals had a purpose—atonement.

The question remains: why sacrifice animals? First, remember the apostle Paul's words regarding sin: "The wages of sin is death" (Romans 6:23). Second, keep in mind that the regulations for sacrifices occur in the context of the tabernacle. Animals became substitutes for humans. It was a life—an innocent life—for another's life, the life of a guilty one. Animal sacrifice, then, was God's gracious provision for humans. The shedding and use of the animal's blood for the purifying or atoning rituals was a reminder for the worshiper that a life had been taken. The cost of sin is high indeed. The sacrifice of an animal allowed the Israelites to dwell alongside God himself as his presence dwelt in the tabernacle.

Four Kinds of Sacrifice in the Old Testament

SACRIFICE	DESCRIPTION
SIN OFFERING AND GUILT OFFERING Leviticus 4–6:1–7, 24–30; 7:1–10	• Sin offerings atoned for sins against God. • Guilt offerings addressed sins against others and included paying damages with interest. • Various animals were offered, depending on the person's position and income. Priests, as examples to others, had to offer larger sacrifices for sin, while the poor offered what they could afford. • Blood was sprinkled on the altar, and certain parts of the animals were burned, often with wine poured on them (drink offering). • Other parts of the animals were roasted for the priests. (Since the priests were full-time tabernacle workers, sacrificed animals were their main source of food.)
BURNT OFFERING Leviticus 1; 6:8–13	• This offering represented complete dedication and surrender to God. • The animal, usually an unblemished male, bore the worshiper's sins and died in his or her place. • After the blood was sprinkled on the altar, the animal was completely burned up. None of it was roasted for eating.
MEAL (GRAIN) OFFERING Leviticus 2; 6:14–23 Numbers 15:1–12	• This offering was given to God in thankfulness. • The people brought fine flour, unleavened cakes, or roasted grain to the priests. • The priests burned a symbolic handful at the altar and could partake of the rest.
FELLOWSHIP (PEACE) OFFERING Leviticus 3; 7:11–34	• This offering symbolized fellowship and peace with God through shed blood. • After some meat was ceremonially waved and given to the priests, worshipers could share in the feast, like a meal with God.

The Laver

The second object in the courtyard, the laver (or basin), was only for the priests. In fact, the rest of the work was performed by the priests on behalf of the people. After making the sacrifice, the priest washed himself at the bronze laver. This washing ritually purified the priest and prepared him to enter the Holy Place.

The laver was made from bronze mirrors donated by the women (Exodus 38:8). While the Bible does not describe its exact shape and dimensions, the laver likely had a shiny, mirrored surface that would help show the priest whether he washed thoroughly. Perhaps seeing his own reflection as he prepared to enter the Holy Place would prompt the priest to reflect on his own need for holiness as he was about to come near to a holy God. For the Lord says in Leviticus 11:44, "Be holy, because I am holy."

What Was Holiness in the Old Testament?

To understand the role of holiness and purity, the following concepts are helpful.

COMMON (ORDINARY)	The natural state of things in the world. It is the opposite of being sacred or holy.
HOLY (SACRED, SET APART)	A special state of being set apart from the common. It is powerful and dangerous when treated lightly. When two priests offered unauthorized (or unholy) fire to the Lord in the tabernacle, they died (Leviticus 10:1–3).
IMPURE (POLLUTED)	There are two kinds of impurity: ritual impurity and moral impurity. Ritual impurity was unavoidable—part of life—and it was not sinful. Moral impurity, however, had to do with sin and disobedience to God.
PURE (CLEAN)	If a person was ritually impure, he or she became pure again through prescribed rituals that might include bathing, offering sacrifices, or simply waiting.
	If a person was morally impure, he or she could face punishment (even death sometimes) and exile; atonement for the sin was necessary.

The issue of purity was very important for the ancient Israelites. The law given to Moses for the people was to instruct them on how to live in the presence of a holy God. The holy and the impure cannot coexist. Yet a holy God desired to dwell with his people who were often impure. Thus, God provided a means to make pure what had become impure. God chose purification rituals and sacrifices to prevent the destruction of the people when they became impure. The tabernacle was a testimony that God was willing to meet with people who strived to be pure.

Live It

A New Covenant

Just before Jesus went to the cross to lay down his life, he shared a special meal with his disciples, which has come to be known as the Last Supper. Anticipating his crucifixion, Jesus used bread to symbolize his body that would be broken and a cup of wine to represent his blood that would be spilled. He said, "This is my body given for you. . . . This cup is the new covenant in my blood, which is poured out for you" (Luke 22:19–20).

This *new covenant* established a new relationship between God and his people. The old covenant—with its sacrificial system, ritual purity laws, and so forth—was fulfilled in Jesus. As Hebrews 9:14–15 says:

> Christ, who . . . offered himself unblemished to God, [will] cleanse our consciences from acts that lead to death, so that we may serve the living God! For this reason Christ is the mediator of a new covenant, that those who are called may receive the promised eternal inheritance—now that he has died as a ransom to set them free from the sins committed under the first covenant.

The sacrifices and purification rituals in the Old Testament were done in anticipation of Jesus' ministry. The sacrifices of animals in the Old Testament foreshadowed Jesus, the perfect sacrifice who atones for sin "once for all" (Hebrews 10:10). Because of the cleansing in Jesus' blood that believers have today, the Old Testament sacrifices and purification rites are no longer necessary.

Life Application Questions

1. What stood out to you most as you read about the Old Testament animal sacrifices and purity rituals? Why?

2. Jesus often confronted the Pharisees about what it really meant to be holy or clean. What does this tell you about Jesus and what his new covenant is all about? (Hint: Read Mark 7:1–23.)

3. As Hebrews 10:10 says, "we have been made holy" because of Jesus' sacrifice of himself. Why was the death of one man, Jesus, able to make us holy?

4. What are some challenges Christians face in living holy and pure lives in our modern society? What challenges do you face?

5. What might living in holiness and purity look like (or should look like) in our lives on a day-to-day basis?

6. Read Romans 12:1. In what ways can you be "a living sacrifice" for God?

Prayer

Jesus,

We stand in awe of your perfect sacrifice for us. We thank you. We praise you. We accept the free gift of forgiveness of our sins.

May we always be grateful that you have made us holy. Remind us that we have been made pure. And help us to live our lives in holiness and purity each and every day.

In your name, amen.

> "We have been made holy through the sacrifice of the body of Jesus Christ once for all."
>
> **HEBREWS 10:10**

Notes

3 LIGHT IN A DARK PLACE

The Lampstand

Light in a Dark Place

The tabernacle structure was covered with various layers of linen, goat hair, ram skin, and other animal skins. After following the proper cleansing rituals at the laver in the courtyard, the priest would enter through a curtain into the first of two rooms in the tabernacle.

What an experience that must have been! A priest would walk from the outside—with the bright desert sun, the smells and busyness of the sacrifices, and thousands of people camped all around the tabernacle—and step into the Holy Place of the tabernacle covered with its heavy layers, separated from the sounds and the smells outside. Here, inside, the priest could smell the aroma of the altar of incense and the fresh bread on the table, and see the flickering light coming from the seven-pronged golden lampstand.

This lampstand served a practical function: providing light inside the Holy Place. But, as with all the objects of the tabernacle, God was communicating something greater to his people through this sacred object.

Read It

Key Bible Passages

Exodus 25:31–40; 27:20–21

John 12:35–46

Optional Reading

Exodus 37:17–23

2 Corinthians 4:1–18

This extra reading describes further the light in the Holy Place and the light in our hearts.

> "I have come into the world as a light, so that no one who believes in me should stay in darkness."
>
> **JOHN 12:46**

Know It

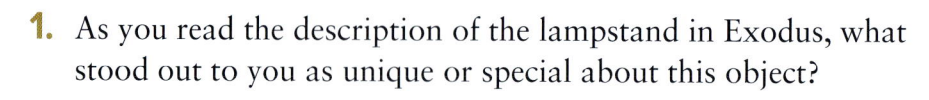

1. As you read the description of the lampstand in Exodus, what stood out to you as unique or special about this object?

2. Why do you think it was important that the lampstand always be lit?

3. According to John 12:35–46, what is the connection between light and belief?

Explore It

The Holy Place

The Holy Place was the first of two rooms in the tabernacle. Inside this room were the lampstand, the table of the bread of presence, and the altar of incense.

This room was considered holy because of its proximity to the Most Holy Place, the place where God's presence resided. It was also holy because God separated this area for special, sacred activities. These activities used objects that became holy because of their nearness to God's presence.

Such holy objects and activities demanded that holy people care for them. Priests had to cleanse themselves and offer sacrifices to atone for their own sins, so they could perform their duties inside the Holy Place.

The Lampstand

The lampstand was a solid, one-piece object of gold that provided light for the priests. God instructed Moses to use one talent (75 pounds, or 34 kg) of gold to make the lampstand. Though we don't know the exact dimensions, it was shaped as a central shaft with three branches coming from each side. Each branch held a cup in the shape of an almond flower soon to bloom, and each cup held an oil lamp. The lampstand was a piece of art!

Although some Bible translations use the expression *candlestick*, the lampstand did not use wax for fuel. Rather, the lamps used clear, high-quality olive oil that the Israelites brought as offerings to the tabernacle (Leviticus 24:2). The priests had to keep the lamps burning continually, probably both day and night (Exodus 27:20–21).

LAMPSTAND	• The lamps provided light in an otherwise dark room in the tabernacle. • Cloth wicks were used to keep the flames burning brightly and continually.
JESUS	• Jesus said, "I am the light of the world" (John 8:12). • Through his life, death, and resurrection, Jesus leads believers to true light.
CHURCH	• Jesus said that his followers were to be a light: "You are the light of the world" (Matthew 5:14). • Having the Holy Spirit as our guide, the church becomes an example of life, a living testimony.

Hanukkah

The word *hanukkah* means "dedication" or "consecration." It refers to the rededication of the temple in Jerusalem.

The miraculous events celebrated at Hanukkah took place nearly 170 years before Jesus was born. Antiochus Epiphanes, the King of Syria, defiled the temple in Jerusalem. He sacrificed a pig in the temple, and he placed a statue of the Greek god Zeus in the temple and ordered the Jews to worship it. This action angered the people. The priest Mattathias Maccabee and his sons organized a revolt and fought a series of battles against Antiochus's army. By a miracle of God, the Jews defeated the army and marched into Jerusalem victorious.

They cleansed the temple, but the supply of oil to keep the eternal flame (the symbol of God's presence) burning was only enough for one day. God performed a great miracle, and the flame burned for the eight days needed to press and purify new oil.

Hanukkah Menorah

For this reason, Hanukkah is also known as the Feast of Lights or Feast of Dedication in the New Testament (John 10:22) because of the miraculous provision of oil for the eternal light in the temple.

In the Bible, What Does Light Do?

HELPS US SEE THE WAY	"Your word is a lamp for my feet, a light on my path" (Psalm 119:105).
OVERCOMES THE DARKNESS	"The light shines in the darkness, and the darkness has not overcome it" (John 1:5).
MAKES US UNAFRAID	"The Lord is my light and my salvation—whom shall I fear?" (Psalm 27:1).
EXPOSES HIDDEN MOTIVES	"He will bring to light what is hidden in darkness and will expose the motives of the heart" (1 Corinthians 4:5).
POINTS OTHERS TO GOD	"Let your light shine before others, that they may see your good deeds and glorify your Father in heaven" (Matthew 5:16).
REVEALS THE TRUTH OF SALVATION	"For my eyes have seen your salvation, which you have prepared in the sight of all nations: a light for revelation to the Gentiles" (Luke 2:30–32).

Live It

The Light of the World

By saying "I am the light of the world," Jesus made several claims:

- He is the very presence of God (John 8:58; 1 John 1:1).
- His ministry consisted of guiding people to the truth (John 8:31–32).
- He brought light and life to those living in darkness and death (John 3:19–21).

In Christ, the full light of God's love and compassion shone forth with power and clarity. Jesus' light reveals our true need for God's forgiveness and shows us the path to God and eternal life. Jesus' light also gives us knowledge of God and his will.

> "For God, who said, 'Let light shine out of darkness,' made his light shine in our hearts to give us the light of the knowledge of God's glory displayed in the face of Christ."
>
> **2 CORINTHIANS 4:6**

Life Application Questions

1. According to God's instructions, the lampstand in the tabernacle wasn't only to be functional (it provided light), it was to be beautiful—a work of art! What might this reveal about God and humans?

2. Jesus came "into the world as a light" and declared that "no one who believes in me should stay in darkness" (John 12:46). In this context, what does *darkness* mean? Why do you think some people prefer the darkness to the light of Christ?

3. When in your past have you felt that you were in a dark time? What light did you need in your life? Did God supply that light? If so, how?

4. Look again at the chart in this session about what light does. Which one of those activities of light do you need more of in your life right now? Why?

5. Read Matthew 5:14–16. Jesus says to let your light shine so that others will "see your good deeds and glorify your Father in heaven" (verse 16). What sort of good deeds would inspire someone to glorify God?

6. In what specific ways can you act as a light in a dark world?

Prayer

Our heavenly Father,

We thank you that you have *not* left us in darkness. You have given us Jesus as our Light.

Remind us every day that as Jesus reflected you, we should reflect Jesus in what we say and what we do. Help us to know how we can let our light shine before others as we go about our daily activities.

In Jesus' name, amen.

Notes

4
GOD'S INVITATION

The Table of Bread

The Altar of Incense

God's Invitation

Across from the lampstand in the Holy Place of the tabernacle stood a table with twelve loaves of bread on it. This table was called the table of the bread of presence—a visual reminder of God's provision and presence.

The third article in the Holy Place was the altar of incense. This small, gold altar stood right outside the veil that separated the Holy Place from the most sacred place in the tabernacle—the small room that contained the ark of the covenant. A special incense constantly burned on this altar, rising up as a sweet aroma to God.

Read It

Key Bible Passages

Exodus 25:23–30; 30:1–10

John 6:25–58

Optional Reading

Exodus 30:34–38

Leviticus 24:5–9

Luke 22:7–20

These extra Old Testament readings give further details about preparing the incense and setting out the bread. The reading from Luke is the story of the Last Supper.

> "I am the bread of life. Whoever comes to me will never go hungry."
> **JOHN 6:35**

Know It

1. As you read the descriptions of the table and the altar, what might these two objects have communicated to the ancient Israelites about God?

2. In John 6, when the crowd sought out Jesus, what did Jesus say they *really* needed to be doing? (Hint: See verses 26–27.)

3. After Jesus declared that he was the bread of life, the people argued among themselves, asking, "How can this man give us his flesh to eat?" (John 6:52). How would you answer this question?

Explore It

The Table of the Bread of the Presence

Also called the table of showbread, this small table was made from acacia wood overlaid with gold. The table was fitted with a gold ring in each corner to hold poles for transportation. The plates and pitchers were made of pure gold.

Each week during the Sabbath, the priests replaced the twelve loaves of bread on this table with fresh bread so that bread was *always* on the table in God's presence. God dedicated the bread for the priests, the sons of Aaron. The twelve loaves represented the twelve tribes of Israel, and by eating the bread, they shared a covenant meal with God. This commemorated the covenant that God had made with the Israelites at Sinai.

In the covenant, God promised to be Israel's King. He would protect and provide for Israel. He would fight for Israel and give them a land. The Israelites promised to be faithful to God and obey his commandments.

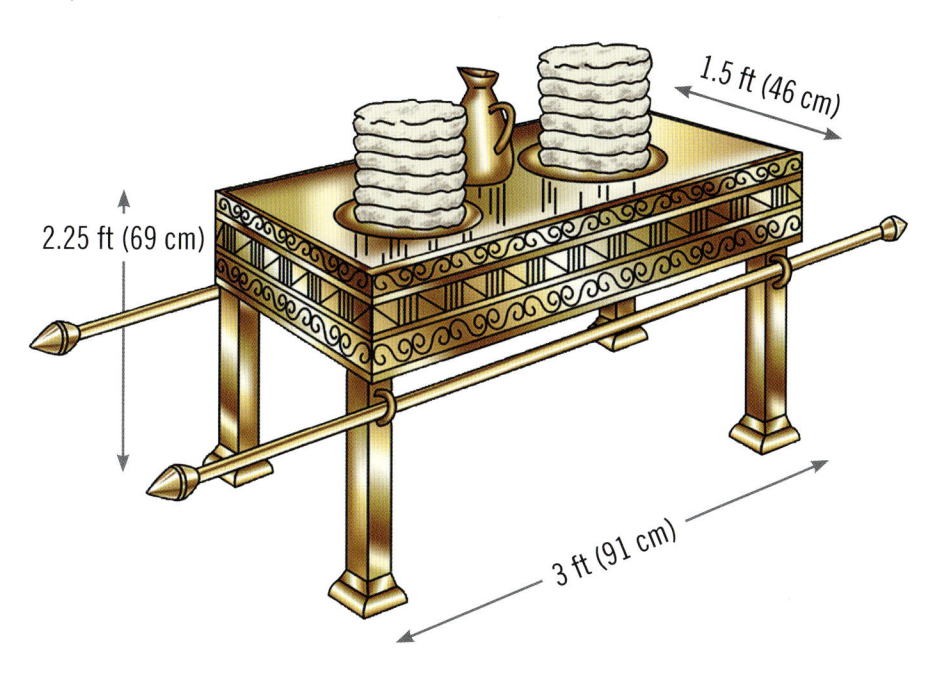

1.5 ft (46 cm)

2.25 ft (69 cm)

3 ft (91 cm)

Bread in the Bible

OLD TESTAMENT	NEW TESTAMENT
God gave the Israelites bread (manna) from heaven to sustain them in the wilderness (Exodus 16:15).	Jesus said that he is the bread of life from heaven (John 6:32–35).
"Man does not live on bread alone" (Deuteronomy 8:3).	Jesus resisted Satan's temptation in the wilderness to rely on bread instead of on his Father's provision (Matthew 4:2–4).
The bread for the Passover celebration was unleavened (Leviticus 23:6).	Jesus warned his followers to beware of the leaven (sinfulness) of the Pharisees and Sadducees (Matthew 16:5–12).
"Give me neither poverty nor riches, but give me only my daily bread" (Proverbs 30:8).	Jesus taught his followers to pray, asking God for their daily bread (Matthew 6:11).
Through the prophet Elisha, God multiplied a few loaves of bread to feed a large crowd (2 Kings 4:42–44).	Jesus miraculously multiplied five loaves of bread to feed over 5,000 people (Mark 6:35–44).
People sealed covenants with a meal (Genesis 14:18; 18:6–7; 26:30; Exodus 24:11). The meal formalized the agreement and bound the people in a close relationship.	The ultimate fulfillment of all covenant meals is the Last Supper which Jesus celebrated with his disciples. In this meal, Jesus instituted the new covenant (Luke 22:19–20).
Bread was one of the things offered to the Lord as a sacrifice (Leviticus 2:4–13).	Jesus used bread in the Last Supper to represent his body, sacrificed on the cross for us (Matthew 26:26).

The Altar of Incense

Made with acacia wood overlaid with gold, the altar of incense stood in the middle of the western end of the Holy Place. It was right outside the inner veil that separated the Holy Place from the Most Holy Place.

The altar had a horn and a ring at each corner. Special poles of acacia wood overlaid with gold were also made.

Priests burned incense at this altar twice a day—morning and evening. The Lord required a special, sweet incense, a recipe of spices to be used only for this altar. No other offering or mixture of spices was to be burned on the altar.

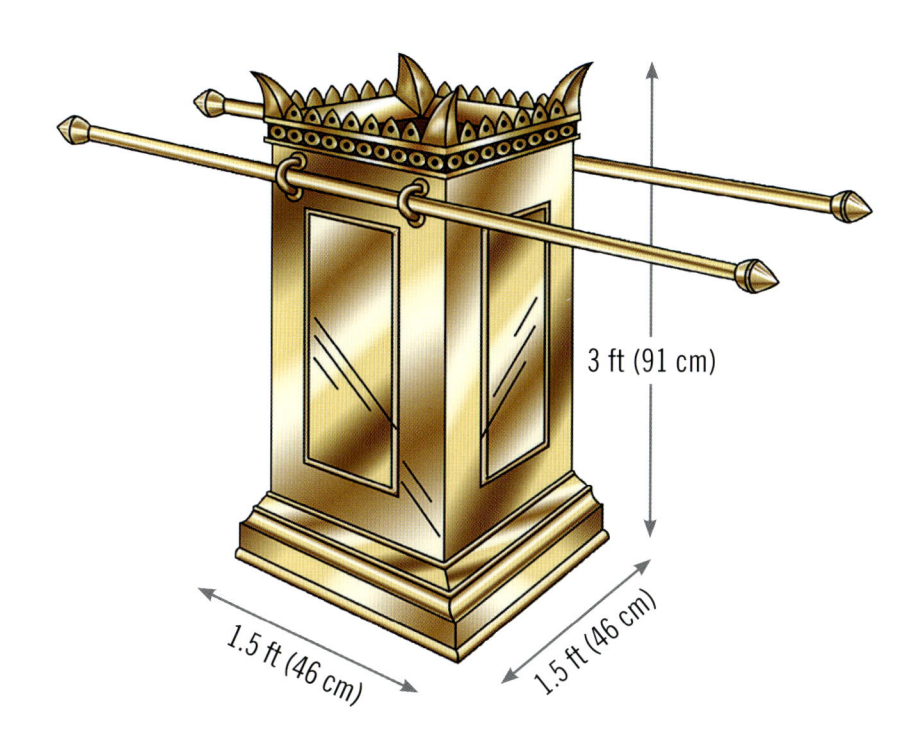

3 ft (91 cm)

1.5 ft (46 cm)

1.5 ft (46 cm)

Like the other sacred objects in the tabernacle, the altar of incense not only had a practical function but also a symbolic one.

PRACTICAL	SYMBOLIC
• It counteracted the odors arising from the sacrifices. Sacrifices occurred daily. The smells would have been quite overwhelming, especially for the priests working in the courtyard. • On the Day of Atonement, the incense that the high priest burned had the function of preventing the death of the priest by covering the Most Holy Place in smoke, so he would not be able to see the glory of God and die (Leviticus 16:13).	• Incense provides a visual reminder of prayer. Just as the smoke of the incense ascended toward God and the aroma pleased the Lord, so the prayers of God's people ascend to his throne and are pleasing to him. • "The smoke of the incense, together with the prayers of God's people, went up before God" (Revelation 8:4) • There were "bowls full of incense, which are the prayers of God's people" (Revelation 5:8).

Live It

A New Covenant Relationship

The God of heaven has offered us an invitation to his table—to be in his holy presence, to feast on his provision for our lives, and to enter into a new covenant with him. In this new covenant relationship, God declares:

> "I will put my law in their minds
>   and write it on their hearts.
> I will be their God,
>   and they will be my people.
> No longer will they teach their neighbor,
>   or say to one another, 'Know the Lord,'
> because they will all know me,
>   from the least of them to the greatest . . .
> For I will forgive their wickedness
>   and will remember their sins no more"
> (Jeremiah 31:33–34).

This invitation is still available to all who open their hearts to Jesus. In the final book of the New Testament, Jesus says, "Here I am! I stand at the door and knock. If anyone hears my voice and opens the door, I will come in and eat with that person, and they with me" (Revelation 3:20).

Life Application Questions

1. Your prayers, like incense in the tabernacle, are a sweet fragrance to God. Why do you think God delights in our prayers?

2. Bread in the Bible was often a metaphor for God's provision. How have you seen God provide for you and others?

3. What specific "bread" (provision) do you need from God in your life right now? Have you asked him for it in prayer?

4. At the Last Supper, Jesus taught his followers about the "new covenant in [his] blood" (Luke 22:20). What does being in this covenant relationship mean for believers? What does it mean for your relationship with God?

5. In Revelation 3:20, Jesus offers to dine—to be in fellowship—with anyone who opens the door to him. When have you "opened the door" to Jesus in your life? If you never have, what is stopping you from doing so?

6. What are some practical ways you can share Jesus' invitation with people who may never have heard that God has invited them into his holy presence?

Prayer

Father God,

We accept the invitation to your table. Thank you for providing for our needs and giving us your Son, the eternal bread of life.

May this prayer—and all our prayers—be a sweet aroma to you.

In Jesus' name, amen.

"May my prayer be set before you like incense."

PSALM 141:2

Notes

5 DRAWING NEAR TO GOD

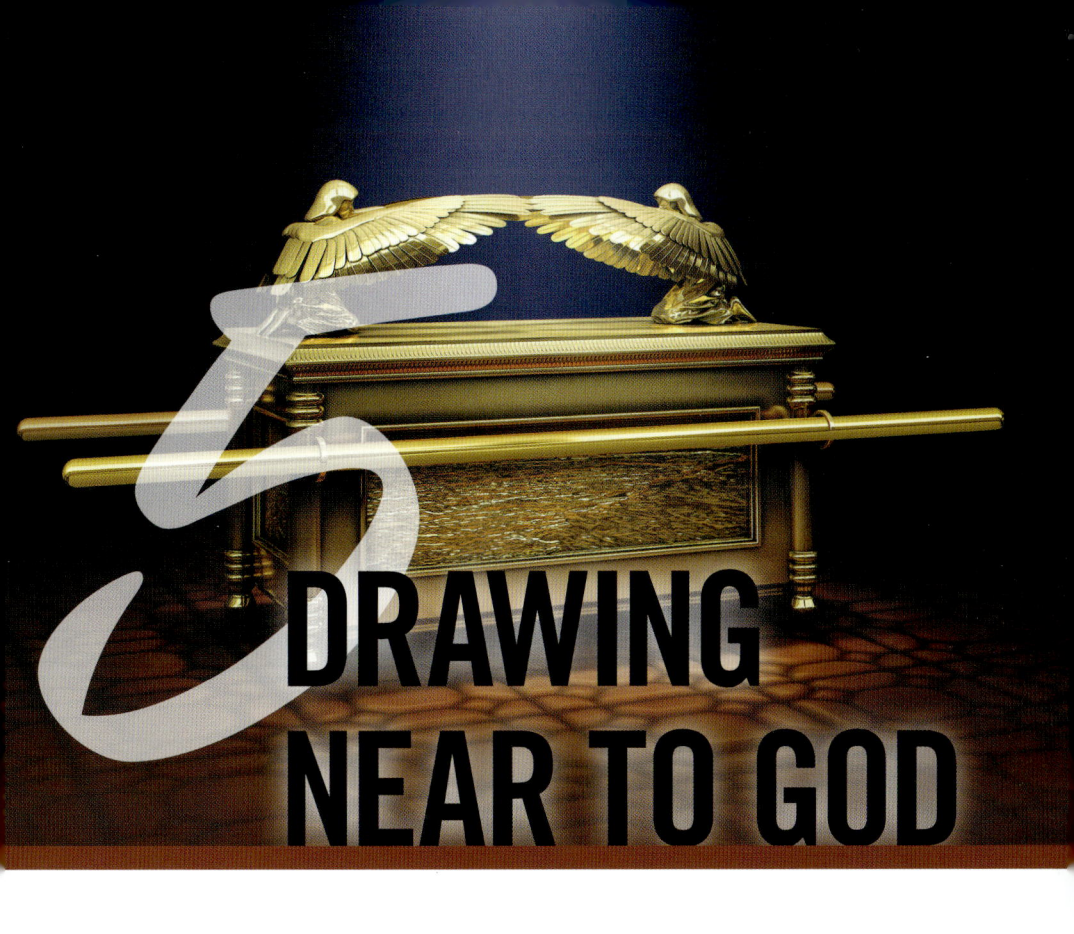

The Veil

The Ark of the Covenant

Drawing Near to God

Standing in the tabernacle, one would have been surrounded by images of cherubim; they were woven into the outer and inner veils and sculpted on the ark of the covenant. These cherubim images hearkened back to the story of when Adam and Eve rebelled against God in the garden of Eden. When God expelled them from the garden—the place of his presence—he situated cherubim to guard the entrance, so humanity could not return. Because of sin, humans had become contaminated, impure. Humans no longer had unfettered access to God. The tabernacle reflected this reality.

Inside the Most Holy Place of the tabernacle stood the ark of the covenant, the holiest of all the objects and the one that most symbolized God's presence. The inner veil, with its images of cherubim woven into it, separated the ark from everything else. This arrangement reflected the fact that that God's special presence was no longer in the garden of Eden; rather, it was in the tabernacle itself!

The holiest of holy places where God's very presence dwelt represented a memory of what humans had lost because of sin. But it also pointed to a hope for humanity—to one day draw near to God as he intended for his creation from the beginning.

Read It

Key Bible Passages

Exodus 25:10–16; 26:31–34

Hebrews 10:19–25

Optional Reading

Exodus 37:1–9

Hebrews 9:1–10

These extra readings describe Bezalel's building of the ark of the covenant and how worship was conducted in the tabernacle.

> "We have confidence to enter the Most Holy Place by the blood of Jesus, by a new and living way opened for us through the curtain, that is, his body."
>
> **HEBREWS 10:19–20**

Know It

1. Where was the ark of the covenant placed in the tabernacle? What was significant about this placement?

2. What function did the veil (curtain) have in the tabernacle?

3. List at least three things from Hebrews 10:19–25 that believers can now experience because Jesus "opened for us [a way] through the curtain."

    • _____

    • _____

    • _____

Explore It

The Most Holy Place

The Most Holy Place (also called the Holy of Holies) was separated from the Holy Place by a thick veil. Although both rooms were holy, the Most Holy Place was set apart as dedicated to God to be his unique dwelling place on earth. Only the high priest could enter this room, and that only once a year.

The dimensions of this room formed a perfect square with each side ten cubits, or about fifteen feet (4.6 m). It contained within it only the ark of the covenant. (According to Hebrews 9:3–4, the altar of incense, which stood directly outside the door in the veil, was sometimes considered part of the Most Holy Place.)

The tabernacle functioned as a kind of royal tent. It was common practice for the king of any nation to camp at the center of his army where his tent could serve as a meeting place for his people. So it was no accident that the tabernacle, also known as the tent of meeting, was placed at the center of Israel's encampment (Numbers 2). God is the ultimate King!

The Veil

The inner veil was a large curtain made of the finest linen dyed in the costly colors of blue, scarlet, and purple. It was skillfully crafted with representations of cherubim upon it. The veil hung on four posts of acacia wood by means of hooks.

By Jesus' day, the tabernacle had been replaced by the temple in Jerusalem. The temple had a similar pattern and also had a veil of separation. Scripture does not tell us exactly what the veil in the temple looked like or how thick it was, but the ancient Jewish historian Josephus described the veil as being embroidered with all manner of flowers. An early Jewish tradition described the veil as being as thick as a man's hand!

Cherubim

Cherubim are angelic beings who do God's bidding and protect God's majesty.

- They protected the garden of Eden after Adam and Eve were cast out because of rebellion against God (Genesis 3:24).
- They surround God's throne (Psalm 80:1).
- Their images were present in the tabernacle and later the temple (Exodus 26:31; 37:9; 1 Kings 6:23–28).
- They praise God day and night saying, "Holy, holy, holy" (Revelation 4:8).

The Ark of the Covenant

The ark of the covenant was the first item of furniture constructed after God told Moses to build the tabernacle. It was made of acacia wood and covered with gold. It was topped with two winged cherubim facing each other. The ark contained three items: the tablets of the Ten Commandments, a jar of manna, and Aaron's staff.

The ark was the only item in the Most Holy Place, and once a year the high priest made atonement for sin at the ark on the Day of Atonement (Leviticus 16). The top or the lid of the ark was called the mercy seat.

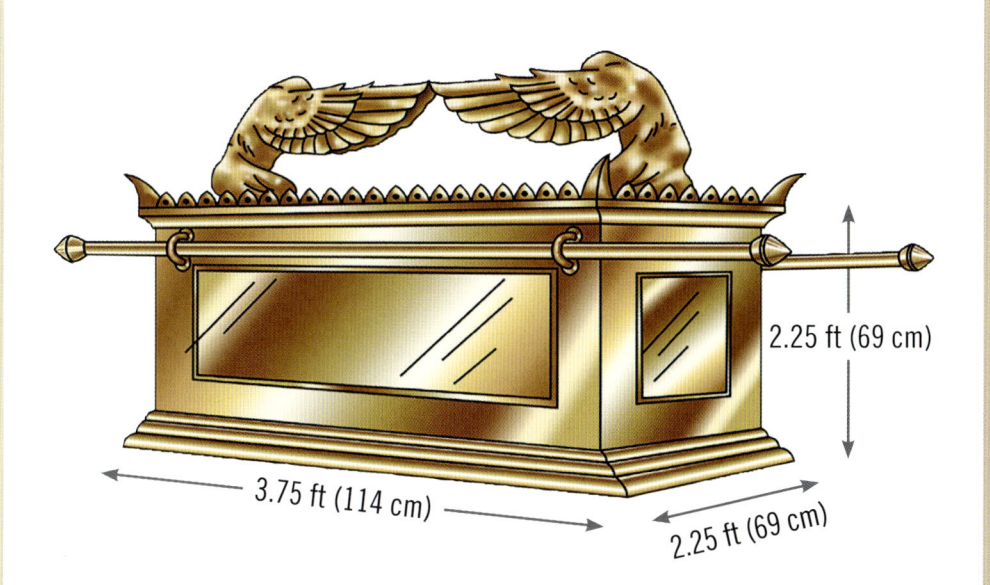

2.25 ft (69 cm)

3.75 ft (114 cm)

2.25 ft (69 cm)

Contents of the Ark

ITEM	SYMBOLISM	JESUS
THE TEN COMMANDMENTS Deuteronomy 10:5 Hebrews 9:4	The stone tablets with the Ten Commandments written by God's own hand were to remind the people of God's laws.	Jesus said that he came to fulfill the law (Matthew 5:17–18).
A JAR OF MANNA Exodus 16:32–34 Hebrews 9:4	The manna reminded the people of God's constant provision.	Jesus is the bread of God who came down from heaven and gave life to the world (John 6:32–35, 48–51).
AARON'S STAFF Numbers 17:10 Hebrews 9:4	Aaron's staff confirmed God's choice and anointing of Aaron as high priest.	Jesus the Messiah was God's chosen and anointed high priest (Hebrews 3:1; 4:14; Matthew 28:18).

Whatever Happened to the Ark?

In 2 Chronicles 35:3, after finding the book of the law, King Josiah celebrates the Passover and then instructs the Levites to return the ark to the temple. That is the last mention of the ark's whereabouts in the Bible.

The ark was probably destroyed in 586 BC when King Nebuchadnezzar captured Jerusalem. There is no mention of it in the list of temple treasures that the Babylonian king took (2 Kings 25:13–17). Nor is it mentioned as being among the several thousand temple articles the exiles were allowed to bring with them when they returned to Jerusalem to rebuild the temple (Ezra 1:7–11).

In 63 BC, when the Roman general Pompey conquered Jerusalem and entered the Most Holy Place in the temple, he famously said that he had seen nothing but "an empty and mysterious space." Although for Pompey the expression was in reference to images of God, it implies that the ark was absent as well.

Although over the centuries there have been claims that the ark survived, no concrete evidence of its existence has been found—but the stories abound. One story says that the prophet Jeremiah hid the ark in a cave on Mt. Nebo, which is east of the Dead Sea in today's Jordan. An Ethiopian legend has Menelik, King Solomon's son by the Queen of Sheba, carrying the ark to Ethiopia while a replica of the ark was left behind in Jerusalem. It's also been alleged that the ark was hid in a church in the city of Axum, where it has been protected by generations of monks.

Yet for all the tales and expeditions, the whereabouts of the ark—or whether it even still exists at all—remains a mystery.

Live It

A New and Living Way

The tabernacle, the place of God's presence, was a visual reminder to the ancient Israelites that God wanted to dwell among them. Yet the sanctuary—with all its coverings, veils, and specific rituals required for entrance—also conveyed a message of separation. God is holy, separate from the sinfulness of human beings. God's presence was there with them, but it was behind a veil. It reminded the people that sin, like the veil, separates all humanity from God.

Then Jesus came to earth and changed this. At the moment of his death on the cross, the temple's veil was miraculously torn in two (Matthew 27:51). The writer of the book of Hebrews compares the veil to Jesus' body torn on the cross so that "a new and living way" might be open to us (10:20). Jesus, who had no sin, became the sin offering for all humanity (2 Corinthians 5:21). Jesus' sacrifice is God's solution to the basic human problem of separation from God. Because of Jesus, the way to God is again open. Humanity, once again, can dwell in the presence of their Creator. We can now have, as the writer of Hebrews declares, "confidence to enter the Most Holy Place" (10:19)—the very throne room of almighty God!

Life Application Questions

1. In what ways does sinfulness separate people from God?

2. Tabernacle activities reminded the people that God's holiness and their sinfulness were not to be taken lightly. What are some things believers do today (in worship, church, and prayer) to remind them of this?

3. James 4:8 says, "Draw near to God, and he will draw near to you" (ESV). How have you seen this to be true?

4. If a fellow believer were to ask you, "How can I possibly draw near to Almighty God?" how would you answer?

5. Have you faced times in your life when you didn't feel confident in approaching God? What happened and how did you respond in those instances?

6. Think of someone who might need reassurance (or hear for the first time) that Jesus is God's solution to separation from God. What can you do to "spur [that person] on toward love and good deeds" (Hebrews 10:24)?

Prayer

Our holy God,

By the sacrifice of Jesus on the cross, we draw near to you now in prayer. Draw near to us as you have promised in your Word. We praise you for making a way for us to come into your presence.

Remind us of your holiness. Forgive us of our sins. Bless us with all heavenly blessings that we might encourage one another to greater love and good deeds.

In Jesus' name, amen.

"Let us draw near to God with a sincere heart and with the full assurance that faith brings."

HEBREWS 10:22

Notes

Notes

FINDING MERCY

The High Priest

The Mercy Seat

Finding Mercy

The tabernacle must have been a place of great mystery for the ancient Israelites. Even the priests did not know everything about this holy place.

In fact, only one man, the high priest, could enter the innermost sanctum—the Most Holy Place—and that, only once a year on the Day of Atonement. It was a place where God's powerful presence was visible—the glory of God! It was a place where the high priest brought blood of a sacrificed animal to the mercy seat to perform a ritual of atonement for the sins of the all the people.

The tabernacle was a place of awe and wonder!

Read It

Key Bible Passages

Leviticus 16:1–16

Hebrews 9:11–28

Optional Reading

Leviticus 16:17–34

Hebrews 7:1–28

These extra readings tell more about the Day of Atonement and how Jesus is a priest like Melchizedek.

> "[Christ] did not enter by means of the blood of goats and calves; but he entered the Most Holy Place once for all by his own blood."
>
> **HEBREWS 9:12**

Know It

1. What was the purpose of the Day of Atonement (Leviticus 16)?

2. According to Hebrews 9:11–28, what are three things Jesus Christ *is* or *does* for us?

   - _____

   - _____

   - _____

3. When Jesus Christ returns, what will he bring "to those who are waiting for him" (Hebrews 9:28)?

Explore It

The Mercy Seat

The mercy seat (also called the atonement cover) was actually the top, or lid, of the ark of the covenant. It was made of gold and had two golden cherubim on top who faced each other while their wings overspread the lid.

God promised to appear in a cloud over the mercy seat (Exodus 25:22; 30:6, 36; Leviticus 16:2). This "seat" was a kind of portable throne, carried along the poles of the ark and complete with a canopy of angel wings. The imagery this created was of God as King of Israel enthroned on the mercy seat of the ark.

2.25 ft (69 cm)

3.75 ft (114 cm)

What Did a High Priest Do?

- **MEDIATED THE COVENANT**
  God chose the high priest to be the ultimate mediator of the covenant between God and the Israelites. The high priest needed to be of the priestly tribe of Levi and pure in his lineage as a descendant of Aaron. Being the high priest was not a choice a person could make. It was God who set down the regulations for the office (Exodus 28; Leviticus 21:10–12).

- **CONDUCTED CEREMONIES**
  Only the high priest could officiate and conduct certain ceremonies, chiefly the duties assigned for the Day of Atonement (Leviticus 16).

- **FOLLOWED STRICTER PURITY LAWS**
  He observed stricter laws of purity than the people and even the regular priests (Leviticus 4:1–12; 21:10–15).

- **OVERSAW OTHER PRIESTS**
  He was in charge of the entire priestly order and involved in supervising the priests and Levites (Numbers 3; 8:14–19).

The Day of Atonement

On the Day of Atonement (Yom Kippur), the high priest made atonement, or reparation, for the sins of all the Israelites. This day was (and still is) the most solemn Jewish holy day. In Hebrew, *yom* means "day" and *kippur* means "atonement" or "covering." Atonement is God's way to bring reconciliation and restoration in regard to human sin and its effects.

Before the high priest entered the Most Holy Place, he bathed himself and sacrificed a bull as a sin offering for himself and his family. He sprinkled some of the bull's blood on the ark of the covenant.

In the courtyard, he took two goats. One goat was sacrificed for the Israelites' sins and its blood sprinkled on the ark. As God told Moses, who was to tell the Israelites:

> The life of a creature is in the blood, and I have given it to you to make atonement for yourselves on the altar; it is the blood that makes atonement for one's life (Leviticus 17:11).

This concept is echoed in the New Testament: "Without the shedding of blood there is no forgiveness" (Hebrews 9:22).

After the sacrifice of the first goat, the high priest next placed his hands on the other goat's head. He prayed, asking for God's forgiveness for all the sins of the people. The sins were thus transferred onto the goat, which was released into the wilderness. This *scapegoat* carried Israel's sins away, never to return.

Old Covenant & New Covenant

SACRIFICE	OLD COVENANT	NEW COVENANT
TYPE	Blood of animals (Exodus 12:5)	Blood of Jesus (Hebrews 9:12; 10:19; 13:12)
QUALITY	Not enough (Hebrews 10:4)	Enough (Hebrews 9:26)
QUANTITY	Many times (Hebrews 10:1)	Just once (Hebrews 9:27–28)
EFFECTIVENESS	For a day or year (Exodus 30:10)	Forever (Romans 6:10; Hebrews 9:12)

Yom Kippur Today

Observed usually in September or October, Yom Kippur is a day of fasting. No work is done on this day, including at home. Many Jewish people spend the day at synagogue, praying for forgiveness of their sins. The book of Jonah is read during the afternoon service as a reminder of God's mercy. Often after the evening service, there is a "break fast" meal. The ten days between Rosh Hashanah and Yom Kippur are known as the Days of Repentance.

Live It

Our Great High Priest

As high priests in the Old Testament acted as mediators of the old covenant between God and the Israelites, Jesus is the High Priest who is the mediator of the new covenant between God and all his people.

The high priests under the old covenant offered the blood of animals to atone for sin, over and over again, every year. Now here is what's so amazing about Jesus as High Priest: our High Priest didn't offer another's blood for atonement. Our High Priest climbed upon the mercy seat of the cross and offered his own life—his own blood—as the atonement for our sins once and for all. Jesus is both the High Priest and the sacrifice! He alone was able to become the perfect sacrifice and mediator before God's merciful throne in the very presence of God.

So what does that mean for how we should live today? Take to heart what the author of Hebrews says:

> Therefore, since we have a great high priest who has ascended into heaven, Jesus the Son of God, let us hold firmly to the faith we profess. For we do not have a high priest who is unable to empathize with our weaknesses, but we have one who has been tempted in every way, just as we are—yet he did not sin. Let us then approach God's throne of grace with confidence, so that we may receive mercy and find grace to help us in our time of need (Hebrews 4:14–16).

Life Application Questions

1. Even though Jesus is the great High Priest, why can we still relate to him on a human level? (Hint: Read Hebrews 4:15.)

2. Though Jesus made the *final* atonement for our sins, why do believers in Jesus sometimes feel as if their sins have not been forgiven? Have you ever struggled with feeling forgiven?

3. Hebrews 4:16 says that we find mercy and grace "in our time of need." What's a time when you've seen God generously bestow his mercy and grace in a time of need?

4. In what specific areas of your life do you need more of God's mercy, grace, and forgiveness right now?

5. Ephesians 5:1 says that we should be imitators of God. In what practical ways can you better reflect God's mercy to others?

6. As you consider all you've learned about the tabernacle over the past six sessions, what impressed you most? How has it changed your views or feelings?

Prayer

Jesus, our great High Priest,

We trust in you as the one mediator between us and God the Father. We praise you for the grace, the mercy, and the forgiveness you have made possible through your sacrificial atonement. We stand in awe of you!

Help us to hold firmly to the faith we profess, no matter what tries to shake our trust in you. Remind us daily to be people of mercy, showing grace to everyone we meet, following your example.

In your name, amen.

> "God presented Christ as a sacrifice of atonement, through the shedding of his blood—to be received by faith."
>
> **ROMANS 3:25**

Notes

LEADER'S GUIDE

"Encourage one another and build each other up."

1 THESSALONIANS 5:11

Leader's Guide

Congratulations! You've either decided to lead a Bible study, or you're thinking hard about it. Guess what? God does big things through small groups. When his people gather together, open his Word, and invite his Spirit to work, their lives are changed!

Do you feel intimidated yet?

Be comforted by this: even the great apostle Paul felt "in over his head" at times. When he went to Corinth to help people grasp God's truth, he admitted he was overwhelmed: "I came to you in weakness with great fear and trembling" (1 Corinthians 2:3). Later he wondered, "Who is adequate for such a task as this?" (2 Corinthians 2:16 NLT).

Feelings of inadequacy are normal; every leader has them. What's more, they're actually healthy. They keep us dependent on the Lord. It is in our times of greatest weakness that God works most powerfully. The Lord assured Paul, "My grace is sufficient for you, for my power is made perfect in weakness" (2 Corinthians 12:9).

The Goal

What is the goal of a Bible study group? Listen as the apostle Paul speaks to Christians:

- "Oh, my dear children! I feel as if I'm going through labor pains for you again, and they will continue until *Christ is fully developed in your lives*" (Galatians 4:19 NLT, emphasis added).

- "For God knew his people in advance, and he chose them *to become like his Son*" (Romans 8:29 NLT, emphasis added).

Do you see it? God's ultimate goal for us is that we would become like Jesus Christ. This means a Bible study is not about filling our heads with more information. Rather, it is about undergoing transformation. We study and apply God's truth so that it will reshape our hearts and minds, and so that, over time we will become more and more like Jesus.

Paul said, "The purpose of my instruction is that all believers would be filled with love that comes from a pure heart, a clear conscience, and genuine faith" (1 Timothy 1:5 NLT).

This isn't about trying to "master the Bible." No, we're praying that God's Word will master us, and through humble submission to its authority, we'll be changed from the inside out.

Your Role

Many group leaders experience frustration because they confuse their role with God's role. Here's the truth: God alone knows our deep hang-ups and hurts. Only he can save a soul, heal a heart, fix a life. It is God who rescues people from depression, addictions, bitterness, guilt, and shame. We Bible study leaders need to realize that *we can't do any of those things.*

So what can we do? More than we think!

- We can pray.
- We can trust God to work powerfully.
- We can obey the Spirit's promptings.
- We can prepare for group gatherings.
- We can keep showing up faithfully.

With group members:

- We can invite, remind, encourage, and love.
- We can ask good questions and then listen attentively.
- We can gently speak tough truths.
- We can celebrate with those who are happy and weep with those who are sad.
- We can call and text and let them know we've got their back.

But we can never do the things that only the Almighty can do.

- We can't play the Holy Spirit in another person's life.
- We can't be in charge of outcomes.
- We can't force God to work according to our timetables.

And one more important reminder: besides God's role and our role, group members also have a key role to play in this process. If they don't show up, prepare, or open their hearts to God's transforming truth, no life change will take place. We're not called to manipulate or shame, pressure or arm twist. We're not to blame if members don't make progress—and we don't get the credit when they do. We're mere instruments in the hands of God.

> "I planted the seed, [another] watered it, but God has been making it grow. So neither the one who plants nor the one who waters is anything, but only God, who makes things grow."
>
> **1 CORINTHIANS 3:6–7**

Leader Myths and Truths

Many people assume that a Bible study leader should:

- Be a Bible scholar.
- Be a dynamic communicator.
- Have a big, fancy house to meet in.
- Have it all together—no doubts, bad habits, or struggles.

These are myths—even outright lies of the enemy!

Here's the truth:

- God is looking for humble Bible students, not scholars.
- You're not signing up to give lectures, you're agreeing to facilitate discussions.
- You don't need a palace, just a place where you can have uninterrupted discussions. (Perhaps one of your group members will agree to host your study.)
- Nobody has it all together. We are all in process. We are all seeking to work out "our salvation with fear and trembling" (Philippians 2:12).

As long as your desire is that Jesus be Lord of your life, God will use you!

Some Bad Reasons to Lead a Group

- You want to wow others with your biblical knowledge.

  "Love . . . does not boast, it is not proud"
  (1 Corinthians 13:4).

- You're seeking a hidden personal gain or profit.

  "We do not peddle the word of God for profit"
  (2 Corinthians 2:17).

- You want to tell people how wrong they are.

  "Do not condemn" (Romans 2:1).

- You want to fix or rescue people.

  "It is God who works in you to will and to act"
  (Philippians 2:13).

- You're being pressured to do it.

  "Am I now trying to win the approval of human beings, or of God?" (Galatians 1:10).

A Few Do's

✔ Pray for your group.

Are you praying for your group members regularly? It is the most important thing a leader can do for his or her group.

✔ Ask for help.

If you're new at leading, spend time with an experienced group leader and pick his or her brain.

✔ Encourage members to prepare.

Challenge participants to read the Bible passages and the material in their study guides, and to answer and reflect on the study questions during the week prior to meeting.

✔ Discuss the group guidelines.

Go over important guidelines with your group at the first session, and again as needed if new members join the group in later sessions. See the *Group Guidelines* at the end of this leader's guide.

✔ Share the load.

Don't be a one-person show. Ask for volunteers. Let group members host the meeting, arrange for snacks, plan socials, lead group prayer times, and so forth. The old saying is true: Participants become boosters; spectators become critics.

✔ Be flexible.

If a group member shows up in crisis, it is okay to stop and take time to surround the hurting brother or sister with love. Provide a safe place for sharing. Listen and pray for his or her needs.

✔ Be kind.

Remember, there's a story—often a heart-breaking one—behind every face. This doesn't *excuse* bad or disruptive behavior on the part of group members, but it might *explain* it.

A Few Don'ts

✘ Don't "wing it."
Although these sessions are designed to require minimum preparation, read each one ahead of time. Highlight the questions you feel are especially important for your group to spend time on.

✘ Don't feel ashamed to say, "I don't know."
Disciple means "learner," not "know-it-all."

✘ Don't feel the need to "dump the truck."
You don't have to say everything you know. There is always next week. A little silence during group discussion time, that's fine. Let members wrestle with questions.

✘ Don't put members on the spot.
Invite others to share and pray, but don't pressure them. Give everyone an opportunity to participate. People will open up on their own time as they learn to trust the group.

✘ Don't go down "rabbit trails."
Be careful not to let one person dominate the time or for the discussion to go down the gossip road. At the same time, don't short-circuit those occasions when the Holy Spirit is working in your group members' lives and therefore they *need* to share a lot.

✘ Don't feel pressure to cover every question.
Better to have a robust discussion of four questions than a superficial conversation of ten.

✘ Don't go long.
Encourage good discussion, but don't be afraid to "rope 'em back in" when needed. Start and end on time. If you do this from the beginning, you'll avoid the tendency of group members to arrive later and later as the season goes on.

How to Use This Study Guide

Many group members have busy lives—dealing with long work hours, childcare, and a host of other obligations. These sessions are designed to be as simple and straightforward as possible to fit into a busy schedule. Nevertheless, encourage group members to set aside some time during the week (even if it's only a little) to pray, read the key Bible passage, and respond to questions in this study guide. This will make the group discussion and experience much more rewarding for everyone.

Each session contains four parts.

Read It

The *Key Bible Passage* is the portion of Scripture everyone should read during the week before the group meeting. The group can read it together at the beginning of the session as well.

The *Optional Reading* is for those who want to dig deeper and read lengthier Bible passages on their own during the week.

Know It

This section encourages participants to reflect on the Bible passage they've just read. Here, the goal is to interact with the biblical text and grasp what it says. (We'll get into practical application later.)

Explore It

Here group members can find background information with charts and visuals to help them understand the Bible passage and the topic more deeply. They'll move beyond the text itself and see how it connects to other parts of Scripture and the historical and cultural context.

Live It

Finally, participants will examine how God's Word connects to their lives. There are application questions for group discussion or personal reflection, practical ideas to apply what they've learned from God's Word, and a closing thought and/or prayer. (Remember, you don't have to cover all the questions or everything in this section during group time. Focus on what's most important for your group.)

Celebrate!

Here's an idea: Have a plan for celebrating your time together after the last session of this Bible study. Do something special after your gathering time, or plan a separate celebration for another time and place. Maybe someone in your group has the gift of hospitality—let them use their gifting and organize the celebration.

	30-MINUTE SESSION	**60-MINUTE SESSION**
READ IT	Open in prayer and read the *Key Bible Passage*. 5 minutes	Open in prayer and read the *Key Bible Passage*. 5 minutes
KNOW IT	Ask: "What stood out to you from this Bible passage?" 5 minutes	Ask: "What stood out to you from this Bible passage?" 5 minutes
EXPLORE IT	Encourage group members to read this section on their own, but don't spend group time on it. Move on to the life application questions.	Ask: "What did you find new or helpful in the *Explore It* section? What do you still have questions about?" 10 minutes
LIVE IT	Members voluntarily share their answers to 3 or 4 of the life application questions. 15 minutes	Members voluntarily share their answers to the life application questions. 25 minutes
PRAYER & CLOSING	Conclude with a brief prayer. 5 minutes	Share prayer requests and praise reports. Encourage the group to pray for each other in the coming week. Conclude with a brief prayer. 15 minutes

90-MINUTE SESSION

Open in prayer and read the *Key Bible Passage*.

5 minutes

- Ask: "What stood out to you from this Bible passage?"
- Then go over the *Know It* questions as a group.

10 minutes

- Ask: "What did you find new or helpful in the *Explore It* section? What do you still have questions about?"
- Here, the leader can add information found while preparing for the session.
- If there are questions or a worksheet in this section, go over those as a group.

20 minutes

- Members voluntarily share their answers to the life application questions.
- Wrap up this time with a closing thought or suggestions for how to put into practice in the coming week what was just learned from God's Word.

30 minutes

- Share prayer requests and praise reports.
- Members voluntarily pray during group time about the requests and praises shared.
- Encourage the group to pray for each other in the coming week.

25 minutes

Group Guidelines

This group is about discovering God's truth, supporting each other, and finding growth in our new life in Christ. To reach these goals, a group needs a few simple guidelines that everyone should follow for the group to stay healthy and for trust to develop.

1. **Everyone agrees to make group time a priority.**
   We understand that there are work, health, and family issues that come up. So if there is an emergency or schedule conflict that cannot be avoided, be sure to let someone know that you can't make it that week. This may seem like a small thing, but it makes a big difference to your other group members.

2. **What is said in the group stays in the group.**
   Accept it now: we are going to share some personal things. Therefore, the group must be a safe and confidential place to share.

3. **Don't be judgmental, even if you strongly disagree.**
   Listen first, and contribute your perspective only as needed. Remember, you don't fully know someone else's story. Take this advice from James: "Be quick to listen, slow to speak, and slow to become angry" (James 1:19).

4. **Be patient with one another.**
   We are all in process, and some of us are hurting and struggling more than others. Don't expect bad habits or attitudes to disappear overnight.

5. **Everyone participates.**
   It may take time to learn how to share, but as you develop a trust toward the other group members, take the chance.

If you struggle in any of these areas, ask God's help for growth, and ask the group to help hold you accountable. Remember, you're all growing together.

Notes

ROSE VISUAL BIBLE STUDIES
6-Session Study Guides for Personal or Group Use

Rose Visual Bible Studies are packed with full-color visuals that show key information at a glance! With their easy-to-use format—*read it*, *know it*, *explore it*, and *live it*—these 6-week inductive studies are perfect for gaining a deeper insight into God's Word.

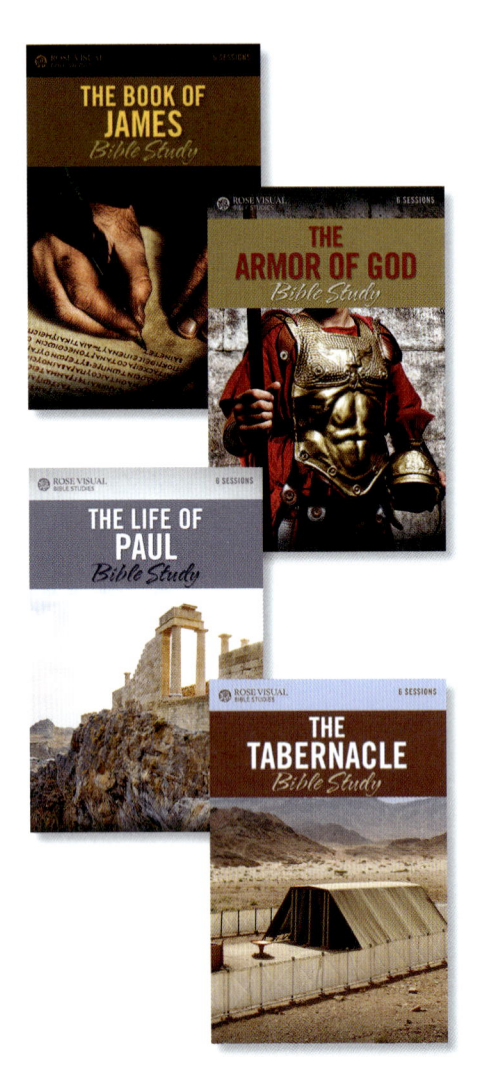

THE BOOK OF JAMES
Find out what James says about cultivating a genuine living faith through six tests of faith: trials, favoritism, good works, speech, relationships, and prayer.
ISBN 9781628627589

THE ARMOR OF GOD
Dig deep into Ephesians 6 and learn the meaning of each piece of the armor, its historical uses, and its application to spiritual battles today.
ISBN 9781628627558

THE LIFE OF PAUL
From his conversion on the road to Damascus to his martyrdom in Rome, see how the apostle Paul persevered through trials and fearlessly proclaimed the gospel of Jesus.
ISBN 9781628627619

THE TABERNACLE
From the golden lampstand to the ark of the covenant, discover how each item of the tabernacle foreshadowed Jesus and what that means for us today.
ISBN 9781628627527

HENDRICKSON PUBLISHERS   **ROSE PUBLISHING**

www.hendricksonrose.com